Welcome Way

A 28-mile route connecting ... ey in Wharfedale and Baildon, with ... ound Bingley.

Editors

John Sparshatt, David Asher & Richard Freeman

Published by the Four Walkers are Welcome Communities

ISBN: 978-0-9564441-5-8

Contents

Walkers are Welcome

Our purpose

'Walkers are Welcome' (WAW) towns and villages across the UK are places that have something special to offer walkers of all ages and ability, and provide a variety of outstanding walking experiences.

WAW nationally is a non-profit-making 'Community Interest Company'. The nationwide initiative was launched in 2007 to encourage towns and villages to be 'welcoming to walkers'. The network has expanded rapidly and there are now over 100 locations across the UK that have joined this innovative community-led scheme to benefit from Walkers are Welcome accreditation.

WAW aims are to encourage and support towns and villages to:

- be attractive destinations for walkers, with top quality information on local walks
- offer local people and visitors excellent walking opportunities within their areas
- ensure that footpaths and facilities for walkers are maintained, improved and well-signposted
- raise the profile of local areas as attractive tourist destinations
- promote the health benefits of walking and increase participation
- encourage the use of public transport

Otley was awarded accreditation in 2008, followed by Baildon in 2013, Burley in Wharfedale in 2014 and Bingley in 2015. Since achieving our national accreditations, we have between us developed and published twenty-seven, self-guided, fully-signposted walking routes. The 'Welcome Way' is our first joint initiative to create a walking route that links these WAW communities.

Kate Ashbrook, patron of Walkers are Welcome and President of the Ramblers, says: "Walkers are Welcome has grown at an astonishing pace as more and more towns and villages have seen the benefits of accreditation and have come on board. Now walkers know that, if they see the friendly footprint logo, they are assured of a warm welcome throughout the town, a good path network and waymarked walks round about. So everyone benefits – visitors, residents and the local economy."

Our websites

National: www.walkersarewelcome.org.uk

Baildon: www.baildonwalkersarewelcome.org

Bingley: http://www.bingleywalkersarewelcome.org.uk

Burley-in-Wharfedale: www.waw-burleyinwharfedale.org

Otley: www.waw-otley.org.uk

Foreword by Kate Ashbrook

Here is a first. Three Walkers are Welcome towns have collaborated to produce and promote a route which not only introduces walkers to their splendid countryside, but takes them into the heart of the towns themselves. The 28-mile Welcome Way is more than just a long-distance walk; it is a celebration of all that the three towns of Baildon, Burley in Wharfedale and Otley have to offer.

From the breezy heights of The Chevin and Baildon Hill, to the wooded valley of Glovershaw Beck, this walk takes you through fascinating, varied landscapes right on the doorsteps of the three towns. It was no easy feat; having devised the route the towns had to work with three highway authorities and the Nidderdale Area of Outstanding Natural Beauty team to ensure it was there on the ground. Also included in this publication (pages 46 and 47) is information about an 9-mile circular link route to the Walkers are Welcome community of Bingley.

I am confident that the Welcome Way is the first of many inter-town initiatives. As our towns grow in number, they will increasingly be able to forge partnerships which will provide great opportunities for walkers.

The Welcome Way is a fine example of what Walkers are Welcome towns can achieve and is a fabulous experience for all who enjoy walking in our glorious countryside.

Kate Ashbrook is General Secretary of the Open Spaces Society, Patron of Walkers are Welcome and Vice-President of the Ramblers. She is also a Trustee of the Dartmoor Preservation Association and the Ramblers and a past board member of the Countryside Agency.

INTRODUCTION

Welcome to the guidebook for the Welcome Way – a collaboration that began early in 2015 between the three 'Walkers are Welcome' communities of Otley, Burley in Wharfedale and Baildon in West Yorkshire. Bingley Walkers are Welcome also joined the project at a late stage and an extra 9-mile loop around and through Bingley was added to the route. This project enabled the communities to work together by making connections with each of their established self-guided walking routes, and for designing a long distance circular walk that connected the three. Each has its unique historical origins and an interesting story of its own.

At the beginning a small steering group was formed with representatives from each WAW organisation, under the chairmanship of John Sparshatt. A 28-mile route was planned and divided into three sections with numerous access points in each section. Representatives from each community walked out their section of the route, wrote route descriptions and identified improvements necessary to stiles and pathways. It was also decided that the route would make easy links with bus and train connections so that walkers could get to each section of the route and from one section to another. Equally important, the route was designed to pass through the centre of each community in order to familiarise walkers with its amenities, and as a way of boosting the local economy.

The name 'Welcome Way' was chosen to reflect the four organisations belonging to the nationally accredited 'Walkers are Welcome' scheme. The route is supported by the authorities that are included along the entire route: Nidderdale AONB, North Yorkshire County Council, Bradford Metropolitan District Council and Leeds City Council.

This guidebook includes maps and route descriptions for each section of the route. There is also information about each community that includes accommodation along the route, transport links and historical information. The entire route is waymarked in both directions and easy to follow, and it can be done in short or long sections.

The entire route is regularly monitored and the guidebook will be revised as necessary in future. We welcome your comments about your experience of walking the route and about the usefulness of the guidebook. Proceeds from the sale of the guidebook will be used to fund any future reprint and infrastructure improvements to the route.

Please send your comments to info@welcomeway.org.uk

1. Otley Market Square to Covey Hall Farm 2.8 miles

1. Starting from the Market Square, cross the road at the traffic lights down to the Thomas Chippendale statue, then turn right along Clapgate to Bridge Street. Turn left at Bridge Street and follow the road down to cross the River Wharfe by the footbridge, on the right, to reach a light-controlled pedestrian crossing. Cross the road and join the signposted footpath across open land.

2. Follow this footpath, signed 'Six Dales Trail', reaching Kell Beck. Follow the tarmac path alongside the stream eventually reaching a road (Weston Lane). Cross the road, turn left, then right into Weston Drive. The stream, Kell Beck, is now on your right and the path ahead over the grassed area. Follow the path to a road bridge over the stream, cross it and turn left into an enclosed path. Follow this path with the stream on the left. Cross a bridge and turn right at a T junction then up steps to St Richard's Road. Cross the road into the footpath opposite. Follow the path, terminating at St David's Road.

3. Turn right here and follow St David's Road for 300 yards to reach a footpath sign (Six Dales Trail) on the left. Turn left between the houses to reach a metal kissing gate. Go through the kissing gate and head left up the hill and over the field, on a clear path to a small metal gate in the field corner.

4. Go through the gate and head northwards across the field to another metal field gate. Go through this gate and, now on a farm track, head up the field, through more gates, to exit onto an enclosed lane. Turn left and follow the lane to a track junction. Turn right up the hill, into Clifton Village, to a footpath sign, for Askwith, on the left.

5. Turn left here between the houses, to an enclosed path in front of the far end house, to reach a field. Cross the field to a stile, then over the stile and ahead to reach another stile at the side of a metal field gate. Go over this stile and across the field to reach a stone footbridge over a stream and a stone squeeze stile in the far right-hand corner. Go through this stile and cross the track into the field. Cross the field and now, with the hedge/field boundary on the left, continue to enter a copse via a stile. Go through the copse and exit via a wooden gate. Go diagonally left to a double gate, then through the smaller of the two gates and cross Covey Hall Farmyard on the left, to exit, via a gate, into a large field.

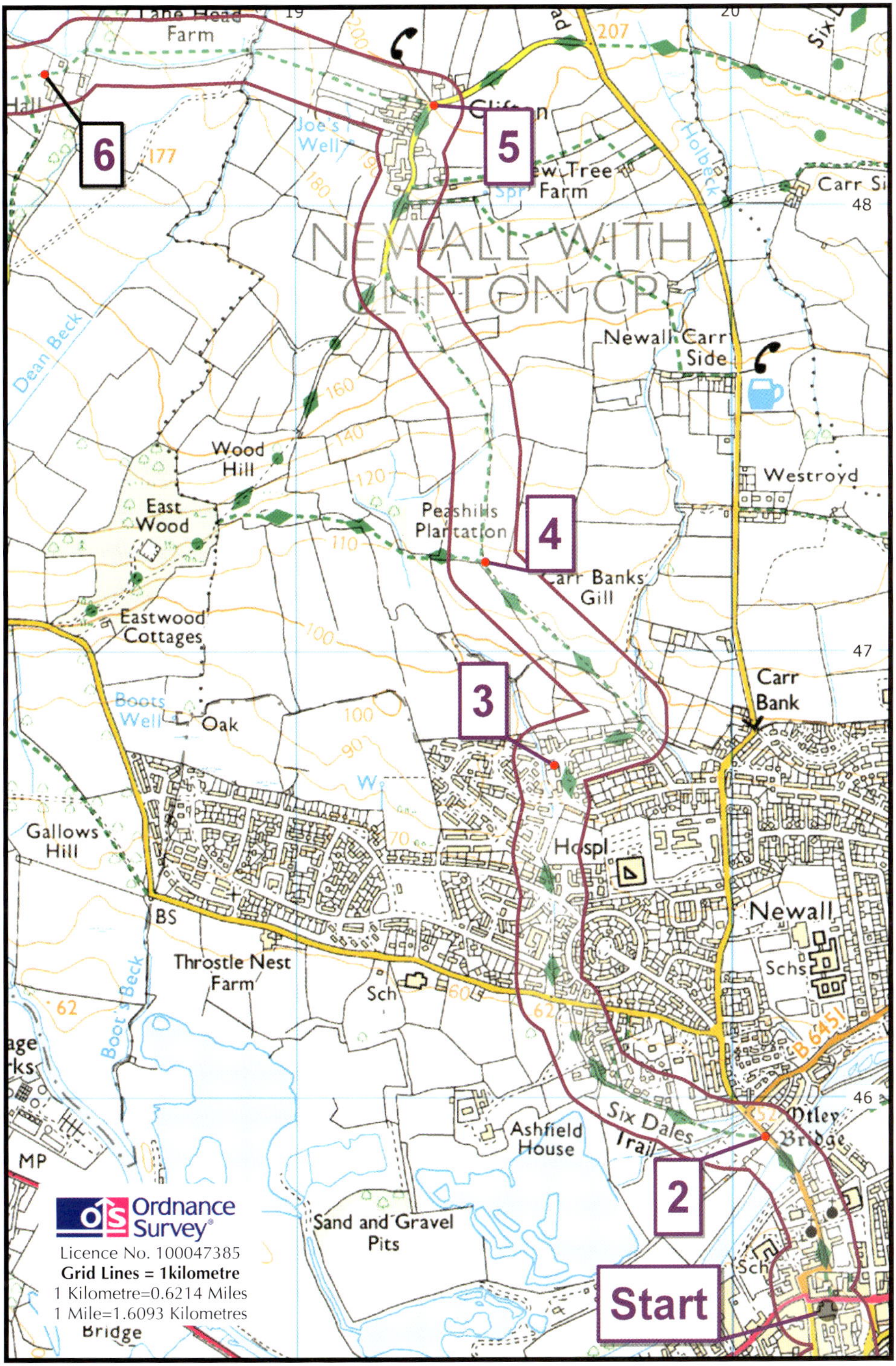
Lane Head
Farm
Hall
6
5
4
3
2
Start
Clifton
Joe's Well
177
200
190
180
207
Yew Tree
Spr
Farm
Holbeck
Six
Carr Si
48
NEWALL WITH
CLIFTON CP
Newall Carr
Side
Dean Beck
160
140
120
110
100
90
70
60
62
Wood
Hill
East
Wood
Peashills
Plantation
Carr Banks
Gill
Westroyd
Eastwood
Cottages
47
Carr
Bank
Boots
Well
Oak
Gallows
Hill
Hospl
Newall
Schs
BS
Throstle Nest
Farm
Sch
Boot's Beck
B 6451
age
rks
46
Otley
Bridge
Six Dales
Trail
Ashfield
House
MP
Sand and Gravel
Pits
Sch
Bridge
19
20
Ordnance
Survey
Licence No. 100047385
Grid Lines = 1kilometre
1 Kilometre=0.6214 Miles
1 Mile=1.6093 Kilometres

2. Covey Hall Farm to Hall Lane 1.9 miles

6. From Covey Hall Farm head slightly south of west across the field, footpath sign to Askwith, to a stone stile near a dog-leg in the wall. Go over this stile and cross the next field diagonally to the bottom right, up to a stile and footbridge in the hedge line. Go over the stile and footbridge and ahead on to a track leading towards Askwith. At the next track junction, turn sharp right and uphill and follow this track to Grassgarth Farm.

7. Immediately before the farm cross over a stile on the left and continue towards a large tree. Head across the field ahead, just south of west, downhill to a fence and follow this fence around the corner to a stile. Go over this stile and follow the field edge, on the right, to a hidden stone stile in a wall at the overgrown field corner. Go over this stile and, keeping the field boundary on the right, go through a metal gate approaching the farm buildings just before Askwith. Go through the gates in the farm yard and down to the ford across East Beck. Cross the beck and up the track to the road in Askwith. (If stock blocks the path then go around the barn on the left and re-join the farm track.)

8. On reaching the road at Town Head (SE 172486) turn left downhill for 100 yds. Then turn right onto a footpath, by a timber-clad garage and go through a gate. Follow the footpath past the caravan storage field into field. Carry on along the right-hand side of this field to a stile. Turn left here before another stile, past some stone blocks and follow the footpath to cross a stone stile by a large ash tree and then pass the ponds to your right. Go straight ahead, with a small, fenced wood on your right towards a large wood and at the right corner of the wood as you near it, a short rough track appears downhill to cross Picketts Beck to reach Hall Lane (SE 164494).

Stile leading to Hall Lane

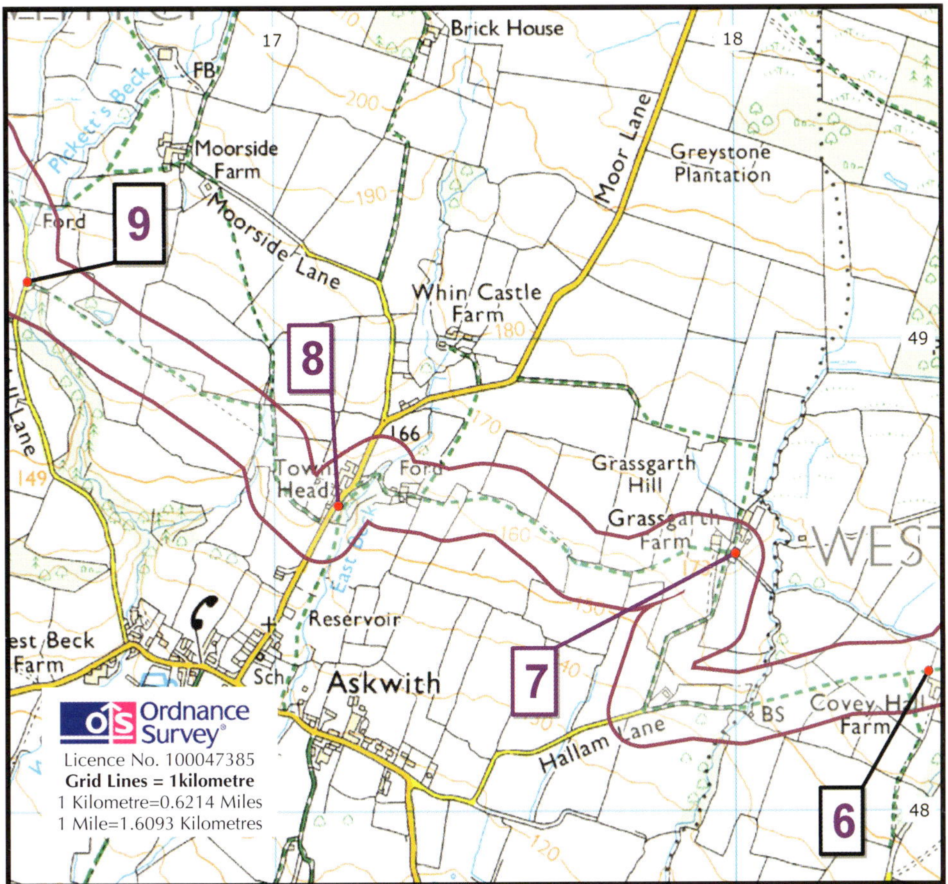

Track near Scales Gill

3. Hall Lane to Denton 2.6 miles

9. Turn right up Hall Lane on tarmac towards a gravel track, continuing on past Scales House Farm. At the start of a conifer plantation on the left there is a convenient seat by the wall on the right. Carry on past Scots Pines at the end of the plantation and, where the track turns sharp right uphill, go straight on over a wall stile adjacent to a gate, then over a ladder stile. Follow the wall then fence on the right to reach the valley bottom diagonally to the left to reach a gate. Go through the gate and in 40 yds cross an attractive stone bridge over Hundwith Beck. Follow footpath signs through the wood. At the top of the steepest part of bank, the path turns right to meet a ladder stile at the edge of the wood which leads into a large field.

10. Cross this stile and go over the field to the right of a wall with a fence on your left. On reaching the brow of a slight hill, bear right to reach a ladder stile at the wall end, cross it and head diagonally right down across a field to the corner of a conifer plantation. Follow the track with the plantation on your left, turn right by a wall following the track and then left over a cattle grid to proceed down tarmacked Smithy Lane for almost a mile to a T junction at Denton (SE 144490).

Hundwith Beck

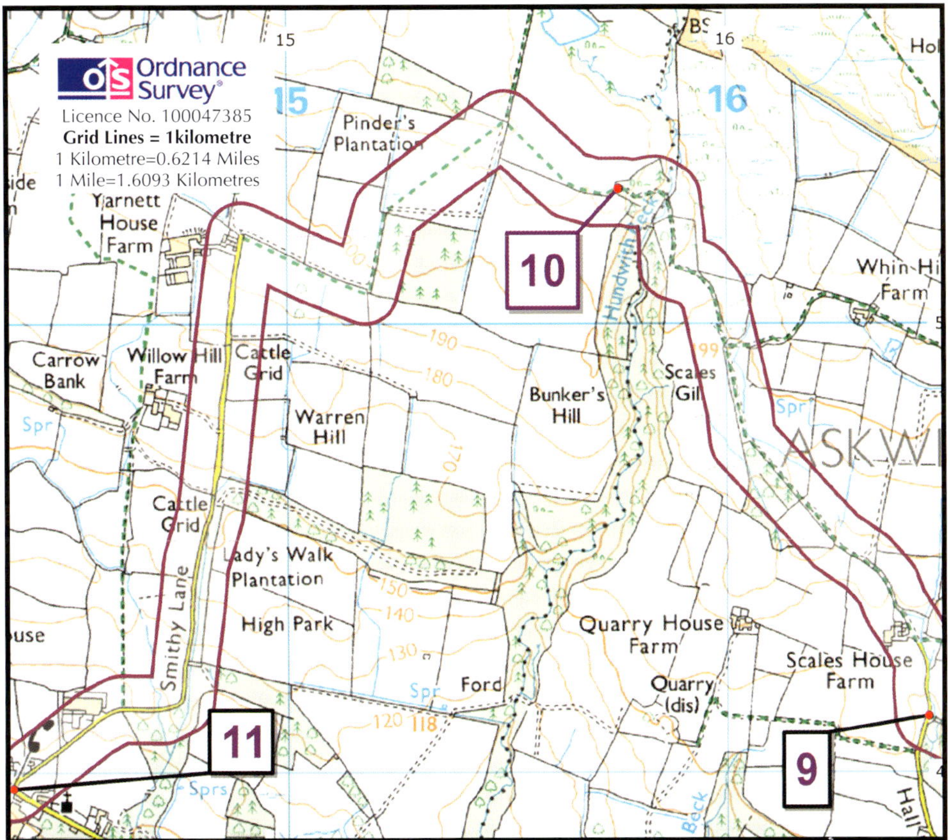

Denton Church

4. Denton to Sun Lane Rail Crossing 3.4 miles.

11. At the T junction turn right and almost immediately turn left into Denton Road. At the bottom of the hill, where the road turns left, take the footpath on the track to the right, keeping straight on to the left of the woodland. Where the track turns right, go straight ahead. Cross the stile and carry on where a wall comes in from the left and look out for a gate and stile at the wall end. Go through the gate or stile and head diagonally left to a metal gate across a small field then follow the path through Beckfoot Farm and over Bow Beck. Proceed along the farm access road to meet Carter's lane. Turn left and left again at the T junction with Denton Road, running adjacent to the River Wharfe. This section of road can be fairly busy but the right hand side has a grass verge most of the way to the suspension bridge. Cross Denton Bridge to reach the A65 (SE 137482).

12. Turn right along the A65 to the traffic lights and then turn left up Wheatley Lane passing underneath the railway bridge. Ben Rhydding station is on the right, with trains to Ilkley, Leeds and Bradford. Take the third road on the left after the bridge, Ben Rhydding Drive, going through the impressive stone gate piers that originally formed the entrance to the Ben Rhydding Hydropathic Establishment. The Hydro was opened in March 1844 and demolished in 1955. Continue to follow Ben Rhydding Drive until reaching the entrance of Audley Clevedon retirement village (SE 143467). Refreshments can be purchased at the Clevedon House restaurant situated in the older building at the far end of the site, which has an attractive terrace overlooking the valley.

Ben Rhydding Drive

13. Turn left in front of the retirement village entrance to walk eastwards along a farm track, crossing over a cattle grid to reach a stile on the right. Cross two stiles and follow the footpath in an easterly direction across the field until reaching a kissing gate. On exiting onto a farm track, keep right. When the track takes a sharp turning right, follow the footpath sign to enter a field through a wooden gate. Follow the field boundary straight ahead, crossing three stiles and then the footpath to a metal gate.
Follow the footpath down the field passing Catton Wood on the left and with Burley in Wharfedale now in view. At the bottom of the hill carefully cross over the railway line at the level crossing (SE 156464), which has good visibility in both directions.

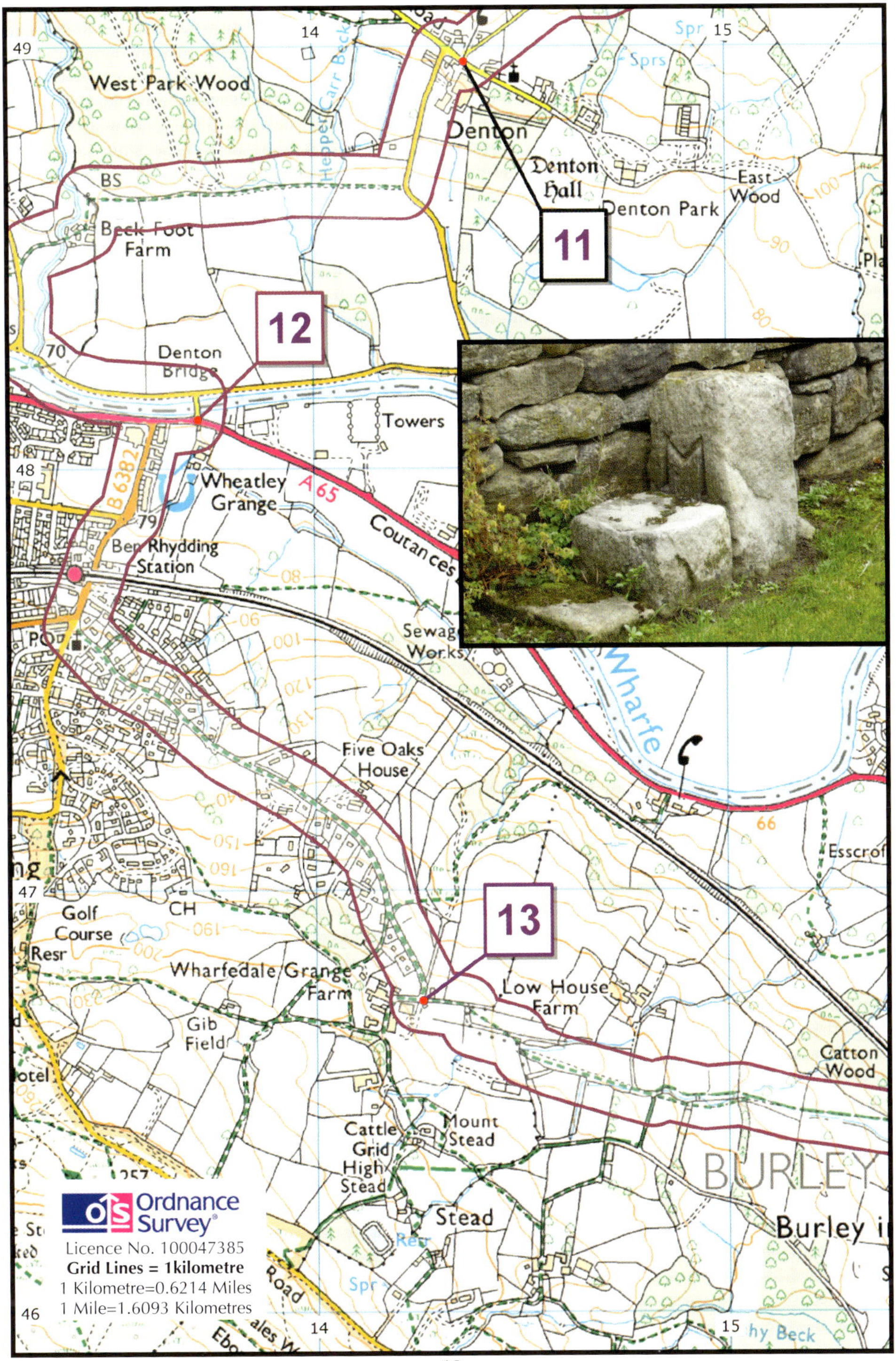

West Park Wood
Hepper Carr Beck
Denton
Denton Hall
Denton Park
East Wood
11
BS
Beck Foot Farm
12
Denton Bridge
Towers
Wheatley Grange
A 65
Couttances
B 6382
Ben Rhydding Station
PO
Sewage Works
Wharfe
Five Oaks House
Esscroft
Golf Course
Resr
CH
13
Wharfedale Grange Farm
Low House Farm
Gib Field
Catton Wood
Cattle Grid
Mount Stead
High Stead
Stead
BURLEY
Burley i
Hotel
hy Beck
Ordnance Survey
Licence No. 100047385
Grid Lines = 1kilometre
1 Kilometre=0.6214 Miles
1 Mile=1.6093 Kilometres

Welcome to Burley in Wharfedale

Introduction

Burley in Wharfedale is a community of around 6,500 people and lies on the River Wharfe mid-way between Ilkley and Otley. With its associated hamlets of Burley Woodhead and Stead it covers 4.9 square miles about half of which is unpopulated moorland at a height of 300 metres and above. A vibrant Village Festival held during the last week in August hosts multiple activities and events including guided walks. Another village highlight is the Christmas Market and lights switch on held at the end of November. Sun Lane Local Nature Reserve on the west side of the village, once the village's refuse tip, is now one of only three LNRs in Bradford Metropolitan District. The reserve is managed by the village's Wildlife Group, and is a riot of colour in the summer months with over 400 plants recorded here, as well as a number of species of butterflies, birds and moths. Burley has excellent footpath access to beautiful countryside in all directions, including Burley Moor to the south and Ilkley Moor to the west. Access to the Nidderdale Area of Outstanding Natural Beauty to the north is currently via stepping stones across the River Wharfe at Leatherbank, although plans have now been approved for a suspension footbridge. The proposed Greenway cycling and walking route would link Burley, Menston, Otley and Pool. The Ebor Way passes close by at Burley Woodhead, as does the Dales Way link. The village has a range of refreshment opportunities, including pubs, shops and cafes mostly situated along the Main Street. There is also bed and breakfast accommodation at the Wheatley Arms, Ben Rhydding and in the village.

Parish Church, Burley-in-Wharfedale

Burley in Wharfedale: A brief history

The earliest mention of Burley (recorded as Burghley) is in a Saxon charter of 872. The Domesday Book of 1087AD mentions Burley as part of the Manor of Otley. The hamlets of Burley Woodhead and Stead together with Burley formed an 18th century township.

The original village was centred on a 14th century chapel, now the site of St Mary's Parish Church. Nearby was a corn mill on the riverside, a manor house (Burley Hall), a smithy and an inn (the Malt Shovel, now converted into housing). The adjoining Pudding Tree Gardens is named after the giant pudding which was distributed here to residents up until 1787. Remains of the village stocks can be seen near the entrance to the church.

Queens Hall

Before the 18th century the village had grown away from its central core westwards along the route to Skipton, now called Main Street. Some of the farm houses and barns from the 17th century such as Dial House remain, and form part of the village's architecturally diverse Conservation area. Other significant buildings include the Grade 1 listed Burley House, built in 1798 by the poet Thomas Maude on the eastern edge of the village. An old moorland track passed near Burley's upper farms, and this became Burley Woodhead centred on the Hermit roadside inn.

Cotton mills were established in the late 18th century leading to the village becoming industrialised. William Fison and William Edward Forster took ownership of Greenholme Mills in 1850 with worsted yarn and cloth becoming the main products. This was the largest water-powered mill in the country during the 19th century, and by 1871 employed over 1000 people. The Goit which powered the mill and now powers a hydroelectric plant originates at the nearby attractive weir and stepping stones.

Remains of other mills can be seen alongside footpaths between the village and Burley Woodhead.

The imposing twin memorials to Fison and Forster are in front of the Queens Hall on Main Street built by them as a school and meeting place for the village. Forster was also MP for Bradford and, as a minister under Gladstone, a great education reformer responsible for the 1870 Education Act which introduced publically funded schools. The successful campaign to retain the railway line during the 1960s in the face of proposed cuts by Dr Beeching coincided with the demise of Greenholme Mill as a major employer, and has contributed to Burley continuing to grow and flourish as a community.

Burley House Field

Where can I find out more?

Burley in Wharfedale village website, hosted by the Community Trust (which looks after many of the village assets), provides comprehensive information about local news, events and local organisations. Downloadable walks are also provided.
Visit www.burley-in-wharfedale.org.

The Walkers are Welcome group has published guides to walks in and around Burley, and these are available in businesses in Burley, and bookshops in Otley and Ilkley. Visit www.waw-burleyinwharfedale.org for more information.

Fountain of Life and Wharfedale Deli

Public transport

Burley is served by excellent bus and train services. The Wharfedale Line rail services from Leeds, Bradford and Ilkley give fast links every 15/30 minutes (one to two-hourly on Sundays) to Ben Rhydding, Ilkley, Menston, Guiseley, Baildon and Shipley.
The railway station is a ten minute walk from the centre of the village. The X84 bus runs every 20/40 minutes along the A660 / A65 between Leeds, Otley, Burley, Ilkley and Skipton, with bus stops along Main Street. The more local 962 service shuttles between Ilkley and Otley via Burley's back roads and Menston, and the hourly X52 and 762 services go to Otley, Harrogate and (762 only) Keighley.

5. Sun Lane Rail Crossing to Holme Park Rail Crossing 1.8 miles

14. Follow the rough track down the hill to meet Sun Lane. The track to the left leads to the entrance of Sun Lane Local Nature Reserve. Turn right down Sun Lane, following it around to the left where it meets the junction with Hall Drive, and continues left until its exit onto Main Street. Turn right to walk through the village centre. Cross over Station Road, with the Grange, Grange Park, the Roundhouse meeting room and Salem Church on the right (SE 166464).

15. Continue down Main Street, passing the Queens Hall on the left. After passing the Methodist Church on the right, cross over Norwood Avenue walking alongside the village green. With the Malt Shovel Hotel (now converted into houses) and St. Mary's Parish Church on the left, turn right into the village green to follow the finger signpost on the left for Burley House Field. Follow the lane past the back of Burley House with a high wall on the left. At the end of the high wall, turn left through a kissing gate into Burley House Field. Turn right across the field, heading for the wooden bridge in the middle. Cross over Wood Head Beck, then turn right to head for the diagonally opposite corner, passing the Burley Community Orchard on your left.

16. In the corner of Burley House Field, cross the bridge at the corner of Prospect Road and St. Philip's Way (SE 168458). Turn left to follow the broad path alongside the beck, passing allotments on the right. After turning left to cross over a bridge, turn immediately right to follow the tarmac path with the beck now on your right. When reaching the end of a cul-de-sac (Jumb Beck Close), turn right to continue following the beck. The path emerges onto Sandholme Drive. Go straight across, following a public footpath fingerpost, arriving at Holme Park Road. Turn right for a few yards then left down a fenced footpath, indicated by another fingerpost. Climb the steps to join the course of the disused railway line. Turn left then immediately right to descend steps to the kissing gate into the open field. Passing through the kissing gate, turn right over a stile to follow the path through the wood, then steeply up a bank, to the railway line. Cross carefully by the walkway (SE 166452).

Sun Lane Nature Reserve

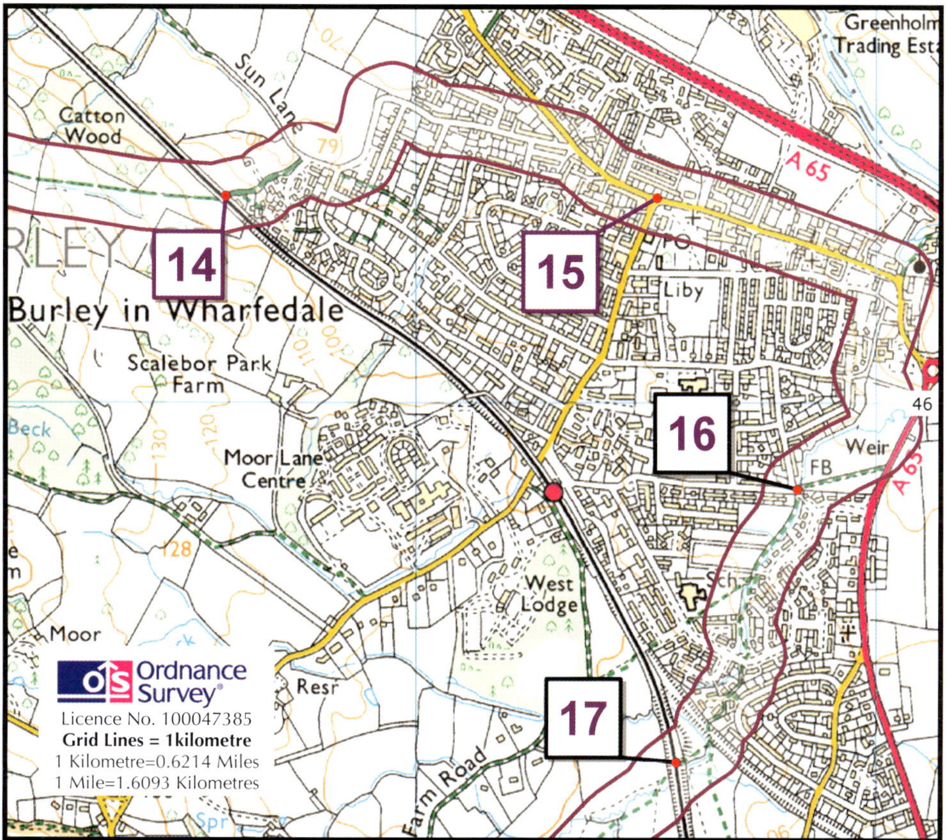
Greenholm Trading Est
Catton Wood
Sun Lane
A 65
14
15
PO
Liby
Burley in Wharfedale
Scalebor Park Farm
Beck
Moor Lane Centre
16
46
Weir
FB
A 65
West Lodge
Sch
Moor
Resr
17
Farm Road
Spr
Ordnance Survey
Licence No. 100047385
Grid Lines = 1kilometre
1 Kilometre=0.6214 Miles
1 Mile=1.6093 Kilometres

Round House

6. Holme Park Rail Crossing to Stocks Hill 1.2 miles

17. At the time of writing there is a proposal with Network Rail to close the crossing and replace it with permissive use of the cattle arch under the line further to the east towards Menston. Any changes will be well signposted. After descending from the railway line, cross the stile and bear left to go through a gate and across a small bridge. Turn immediately right to go through a gateway with a redundant stile alongside. Follow the footpath round the edge of the field with the beck on your right to reach the far corner. Cross a plank footbridge with handrail and bear slightly left to walk alongside the right hand bank of Carr Beck. Go through a metal gate and immediately over a stile. Continue to follow the course of the beck which then disappears underground before a squeeze stile. After the next squeeze stile the beck reappears. At the next squeeze stile with multiple waymarks (SE 159446), the path exits onto a broad track. Bleach Mill House offering refreshments is a hundred yards to the left.

18. Continue straight across steeply up the path with the beck now in a mini-canyon on your left. Pass through an unusual three-stone squeeze stile, walking alongside the wall on your left, passing the site of Middle or Hargreaves Mill and the now silted-up dam. After crossing a further squeeze stile, cross a step stile and go over a bridge to reach Myrtle Grove Mill. Turn up the steep lane to reach Moor Road, Burley Woodhead (SE 156443). Cross over Moor Road and walk up Green Lane directly ahead for 50 yards until reaching a waymark post and then turn left to cross a stream. Follow the path through a 'holly tunnel' to the gate at the end. Turn right to follow the path uphill to a track.

Carr Bottom Reservoir

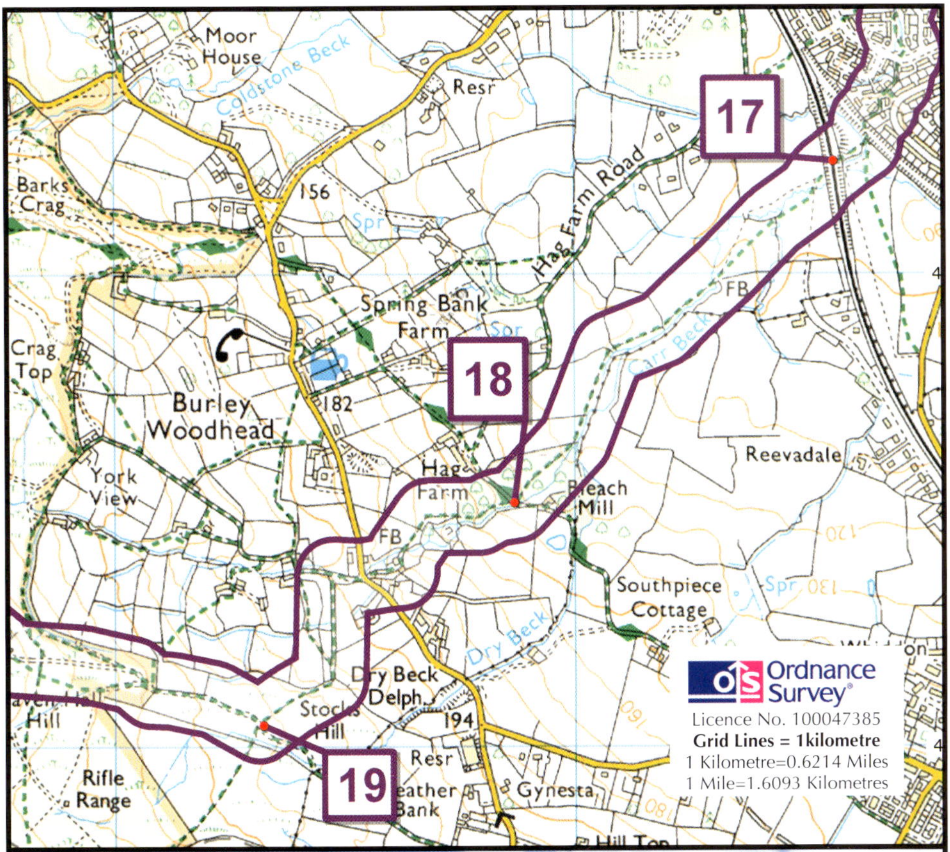

Great Skirtful of Stones, Burley Moor

7. Stocks Hill to Weecher Reservoir 2.8 miles

19. On reaching the track turn right and follow the track to a gate. Cross the stile adjacent to the gate leading to open moor. Three tracks converge at this point; take the middle one, uphill, passing a small brick building and a boundary stone with Carr Bottom Reservoir now visible below to the right. As you continue to climb steadily, views southwards over the Aire Valley towards Haworth begin to unfold, as do views northwards over the Wharfe Valley. Pass Lower Lanshaw Dam below on the right, with the track levelling out, eventually reaching after one mile a shooting hut.

The route here runs along the boundary of Burley and Hawksworth Moors - both part of Rombalds Moor which is recognised for its internationally important populations of ground nesting birds (including curlew, lapwing, golden plover and others) and the habitats which support them. When nesting between March and July, the birds are particularly vulnerable to disturbance so please keep to the footpaths and keep dogs on leads. Wildfire is also a major threat to these areas so during dry periods, take extra care with matches, cigarettes and so on.

20. Turn left after passing the shooting hut, passing Great Skirtful of Stones on the right. Follow the path, signed Millennium Way, through rocks and heather initially due south, with Baildon Moor visible in the distance. Reva Reservoir comes into view in the distance to the left, and you pass a number of grouse butts on the right. After crossing two small streams with boggy areas, the path meets a fence on the left, and crosses over a further stream. Walk alongside the fence to the stone wall and Horncliffe Well, which is accessible over the stile in the fence (SE 133434). This is a peaceful, remote, grassy and sheltered place, very suitable for a refreshment stop.

First described in land records in 1273, the Horncliffe Well traditionally marks the ancient boundary point where Burley, Hawksworth and Bingley Moors meet. The well is described by historians as a holy well or a sacred spring. Water from the well was said to be always plentiful, strongly flowing and truly refreshing. The remains of buildings visible near the well date from 1799, and records including drawings exist of a school on the site in the early 1800s. Close by to the well is Horncliffe stone circle.

21. Go through the step stile in the wall, noting the inscription to Thos. Pulleyn. Turn left to walk south eastwards down towards Bingley Road through a new metal gate. Weecher Reservoir is visible to the right.

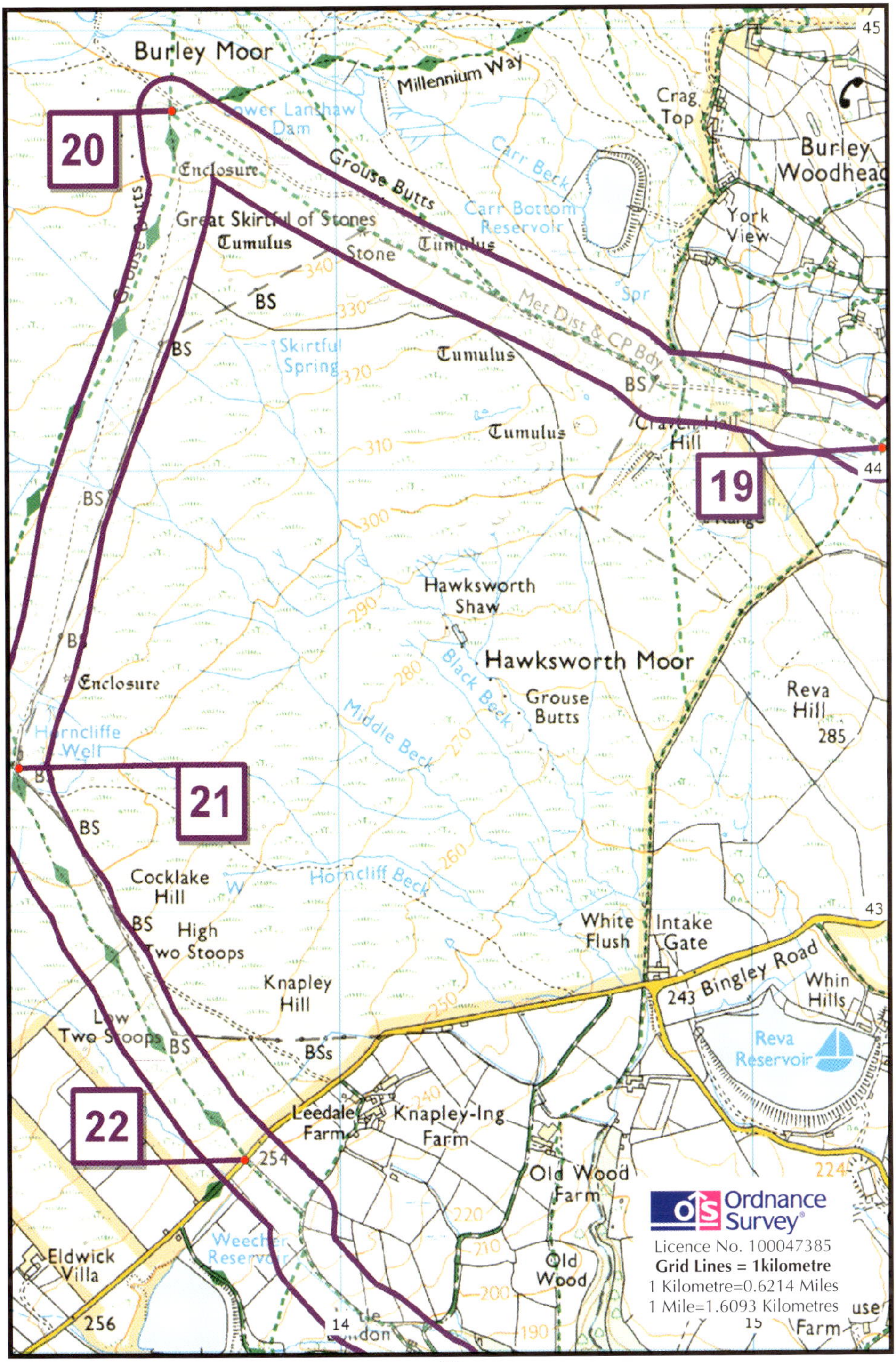
Burley Moor
Millennium Way
Lower Lanshaw Dam
20
Enclosure
Grouse Butts
Great Skirtful of Stones
Tumulus
Stone
Tumulus
Carr Beck
Carr Bottom Reservoir
Crag Top
Burley Woodhead
York View
Spr
Met Dist & CP Bdy
BS
Skirtful Spring
Tumulus
Tumulus
Craven Hill
19
Hawksworth Shaw
Hawksworth Moor
Black Beck
Grouse Butts
Middle Beck
Reva Hill
285
Enclosure
Horncliffe Well
21
Cocklake Hill
Horncliff Beck
High Two Stoops
White Flush
Intake Gate
Knapley Hill
243 Bingley Road
Whin Hills
Reva Reservoir
Low Two Stoops
BSs
22
Leedale Farm
Knapley-Ing Farm
254
Old Wood Farm
Old Wood
Eldwick Villa
Weecher Reservoir
256
45
44
43
14
15
Ordnance Survey
Licence No. 100047385
Grid Lines = 1kilometre
1 Kilometre=0.6214 Miles
1 Mile=1.6093 Kilometres

WELCOME TO BAILDON

With a population of around 16,000, Baildon spreads from the valley of the River Aire, up to the top of Baildon Moor. In spring and summer you can enjoy the vibrant floral displays provided by the volunteers of the "Baildon in Bloom Group" and in December you can marvel at one of the best local displays of Festive Lights, provided by Baildon Town Council in partnership with many local businesses. Baildon is very proud of its excellent Farmers' Market which is held on the fourth Saturday morning of each month. This Market would be an ideal place to purchase items for a splendid picnic lunch for your walk, from the varied stalls selling cheeses, organic fruit and vegetables, cakes, pies, and much more.

Baildon also offers an excellent range of shops, cafes and community facilities. Whilst you are walking through the centre of Baildon why not take the opportunity to rest a while in the Hall Cliffe Community Garden, or visit one of our historic churches. Other notable features of Baildon and its surroundings near to the route of the Welcome Way include: Bracken Hall Countryside Centre www.friendsofbrackenhall.org.uk; the Denso Marston Nature Reserve www.dm-naturereserve.org.uk and Esholt Village which achieved fame as the setting for the TV series Emmerdale.

BAILDON - A BRIEF HISTORY

There is visible evidence, in the form of cup and ring marked stones, that Baildon Moor was populated by a small group of hunter-gatherers some 4000 years ago. Stone tools have been found on the river terraces by the River Aire at Charlestown, perhaps used in winter, whilst the moor was used in summer.

In the Domesday Book of 1086, Baildon was described as being split between the two manors of Baildon and Otley. The village developed with the establishment of the chapel on the site of the existing St John's Church around 1200.
By the early eighteenth century, the village was an agricultural community with a growing textile trade. The clothiers' cottages such as those on Brook Hill and Station Road were built at that time. A network of tracks saw the transfer of wool, yarn and fabric. One track was a paved way which crossed Baildon Moor to Eldwick.

The textile industry in Shipley and Baildon was mechanised between 1780 and 1830 and this led to a growth in housing and population. Baildon grew in several areas - Lower Baildon at Charlestown, Baildon Green, moorland hamlets and the centre of the village around Towngate. With the rise in population came the rise in non-conformist worship. Meeting first in houses, these groups later built chapels, many of which remain, some having been converted into housing such as at Low Hill or apartments such as the Primitive Methodist chapel on Browgate. Others such as the former Wesleyan Methodist and Moravian remain active churches today. For the Anglicans, Baildon became a parish in its own right in 1869, severing the links with Otley which went back more than six hundred years. The Parish Church of St John the Evangelist on Hall Cliffe was rebuilt in 1848, with the tower added as a war memorial in 1922.

After the opening of the Shipley-Ilkley railway line, and the promotion by two prominent doctors of the village as a healthy place to live, Baildon grew. Many large houses were built, including two mansions, particularly in the Station Road area where it was said several textile millionaires lived. Both mansions have since been demolished.

Despite many old properties in Baildon being demolished in the 1960s, it is still growing, with house building in many areas. It retains much of its character though, with two conservation areas: one around Brook Hill and the other up Browgate and along Westgate. There are also some forty listed buildings and groups of buildings.

Potted Meat Stick (Ferrand Memorial Fountain)

The famous landmark the Ferrand's Memorial, known locally as the Potted Meat Stick has stood in more than one place over the years.

Baildon Moor dominates the village and is now a considerable recreational amenity, with dog walkers, runners, mountain bikers, horse riders, golfers, and of course walkers. The common lands were passed down through various manorial families, including the Baildon family, until they were sold to Bradford Corporation by the last Lord of the Manor, Colonel Maude of Rylstone, in 1899.

The moor contains many archaeological sites, the famous cup and ring carved rocks, burial mounds, Iron Age field systems and much more.
There are also many remains of the coal mining industry, including ancient bell pits, now seen as depressions, across

large parts of the moor. There is also evidence of a military presence on the moor, with a rifle range which closed in 1912 and Second World War defences. So when we walk on the moor, perhaps we follow the same tracks as the small number of hunter-gatherers or the miners as they went to work. We certainly tread the same paths as the mill workers who escaped the grim conditions of the Bradford mills to enjoy the fresh air of the moor and Shipley Glen on their Sundays off.

To end, here is a little-known story gleaned from local newspapers. In July 1895 around twenty members of Baildon Liberal Club were apprehended on the Hawksworth side of the moor. The gamekeeper for Mr Fawkes of Farnley Hall accused them of trespass. They went back the following week knowing that a police constable would be present. The Rombalds Moor Preservation Society was formed and on 26 April 1896 around 150 people set off to protest. This did lead to the issue of writs and members of the society were fined a total of £144, far more money than they had. The right to roam and stray was not established on the unenclosed moorland of the Lords of the Manors of Burley and Hawksworth and the society was dissolved. These were brave pioneers, given that the chair of the magistrates at Otley was Mr Fawkes, and it was many years before the right was won all over the country.

Trig Point on Baildon Hill

WHERE CAN I FIND OUT MORE?

Baildon Town Council maintains a lively website which will give you information about news and events in Baildon, as well as guided walks on offer, and routes which can be downloaded for self-guiding. Visit www.baildontowncouncil.gov.uk
If you would like to spend a little more time walking around Baildon and discovering its heritage, download one of Baildon Local History Association's Heritage Walks at http://www.baildontowncouncil.gov.uk/heritage_trails.php or purchase them at Baildon Library.

Hall Cliffe Community Garden

PUBLIC TRANSPORT.

Baildon is well served by public transport with a regular train service on the Wharfedale Line which links Burley in Wharfedale and Ilkley going north, and Shipley and Bradford to the south. A frequent bus service runs from the centre of Baildon to Bradford and the 650 and 653 bus route runs to and from Otley from Shipley Market Square, passing along Otley Road, Baildon.

Baildon also is proud to have an electric vehicle charging point in the Ian Clough Car Park.

8. Weecher Reservoir to Glovershaw Lane 1.7 miles

22. Cross Bingley Road (busy so take great care) and go over a stile following the direction indicated on a footpath sign. Walk down the field ahead with a wall to your left. At a gate at the bottom of the field, turn right and follow the field-wall, passing another gate, as it curves leftwards to bring you to a wooden gate with a stile beside.

Cross the stile and continue ahead following the wall on your left as it descends and curves left, then go over a broken stone stile. Continue to a bridge over Gill Beck on the right. Turn right over the bridge, with a large barn on the left, and follow the track up through two gates, passing a house on the right. Ignore two joining tracks and continue ahead to the hamlet of Faweather Grange. At a track T-junction, turn right and follow the track past a house called Oakwood Barn to your right. Continue ahead on this track, Birch Close Lane, for 0.25mile, to pass Birch Close Farm on your left (SE 138416). Go ahead through a metal gate and continue ahead.

23. You are now entering an area where horses are exercised. As you approach the "horse gallop" cross it and take a clear path ahead on grassland, initially keeping a wall and the "gallop" to your left. Cross the "gallop" when you come to it again and head towards a gate with a finger post. Go through the gate and immediately turn right to follow a wall on the right to a gate and stile. Cross the stile and continue ahead, walking parallel to a ditch and fence on your left. At a wall and gate, turn right and keep the wall on your left to arrive at an old metal gate and stile beside. Cross the stile and pass Golcar Farm on your right. Continue on the track to reach a busy road (Glovershaw Lane).

Weecher Reservoir

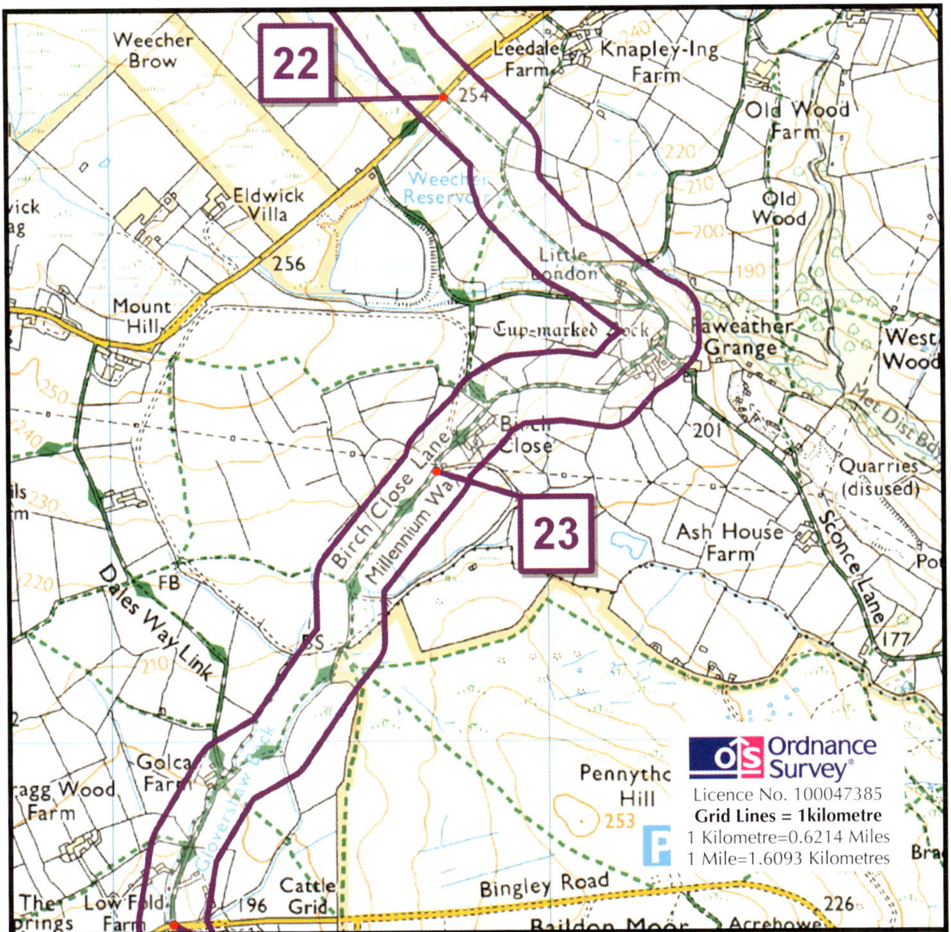

Hawksworth Moor and Weecher Reservoir

9. Glovershaw Lane to Baildon Hill 2.1 miles

24. Cross this road with care and take the footpath straight ahead. Cross a stony stile and follow the path. Continue on a pleasant woodland path with a fence on the left and Glovershaw Beck on your right until you reach a metal gate. Pass through and descend a few steep and stony steps with care to cross a small stream and continue ahead over a small wooden bridge. The path rises away from the stream and you emerge onto open ground through bracken and heather. Continue ahead ignoring cross-paths and tracks to come out onto Bracken Hall Green - a grassy terrace above Shipley Glen, which is down to your right - and soon reaching Glen Road.

25. Turn right and walk parallel to the road. Continue ahead along Bracken Green for 0.6 mile to reach Bracken Hall Countryside Centre on the left opposite an information board about Baildon Moor. Continue a further 100 yards to a signed footpath on the left.

26. Turn left and over the cattle grid to a tarmac access-road around the rear of the farm buildings. By a large barn turn left through a gate into a field and head diagonally right across this field towards a large gate. At this gate cross a stile on your left and go uphill with wall on your right. At the top of this field, turn left to reach a kissing gate.

Pass through and continue uphill with the wall on your right. Towards the top of the field go right over a stone stile (SE 133394). Continue ascending with the wall on your left to pass through a narrow squeeze gate at the top left of the field. Admire a fine view down to Saltaire behind you. Continue rising keeping right, on a clear path, with Crook Farm Caravan Site to your right. On reaching the access road to the caravan site go straight ahead ignoring cross tracks to reach Dobrudden Caravan Park.
Follow the access road for 200 yards then bear right up the path to reach the trig-point on the top of Baildon Hill.

Glovershaw Beck

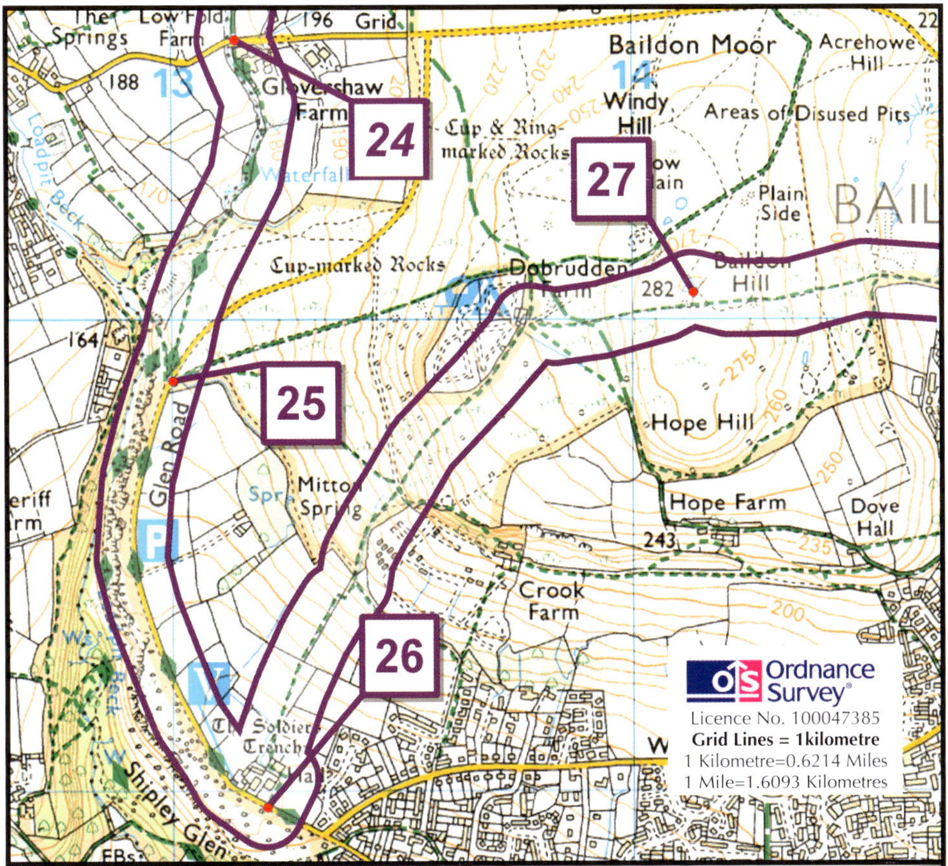

Approaching Baildon

10. Baildon Hill to Tong Park Dam 1.7 miles

27. From this point you can enjoy a 360 degree view: note the diorama which will help you to identify the landmarks you can spot on a clear day. When you have had your fill of the views, head east passing more evidence of shallow coal mining in past centuries, and follow a broad path that descends to Baildon (ignore all cross-tracks). Descend with Baildon Golf Course to your left and houses to your right. As you get close to Baildon, take a right fork to emerge through a gate by Baildon Golf Course Club House. Bear left across some open ground in front of what once served as Baildon Waterworks (inscription on front) and join the pavement alongside Moorgate.

28. Turn right and continue into the centre of Baildon (passing public conveniences on your right) and the Malt Shovel Inn. Note the old stocks and remnants of a preaching cross, before crossing the road at the zebra crossing. Turn right past the Angel Pub and go ahead across Hallcliffe to arrive at "Potted Meat Stick" (Ferrand Memorial Fountain) From "The Potted Meat Stick", walk east up Hallcliffe passing the Ian Clough Hall, Library, and St John's Parish Church on your right and, before long, the Hallcliffe Community Garden on the left. At the mini-roundabout cross Heygate Lane to continue ahead along Ladderbanks Lane. Where the road swings right into Bramham Drive, go straight ahead along a single-track tarmac road with gardens on both sides. When the single-track road ends, at a bench, bear left on to a descending, enclosed bridle path signposted Ladderbanks Lane.

Continue descending along this delightful old lane until you reach a meadow.
Pass through two gates and descend ahead, with the Esholt Cricket Ground to your left.
Go through a gate and turn left along the Dam shore to the end of Tong Park Dam.

Tong Park Dam

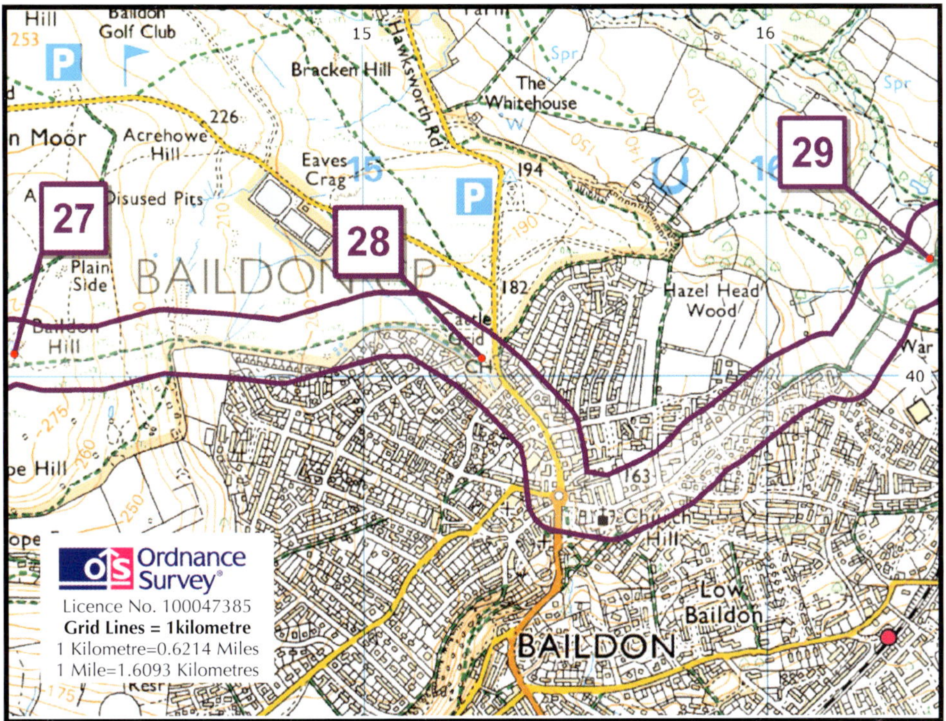

Bracken Hall Green

11. Tong Park Dam to Esholt 1.6 miles

29. At the end of the Dam, pass through another gate and across a footbridge. Turn right and then almost immediately left uphill. Continue uphill with a stone wall on your left and the golf course on your right with views of the Wharfedale Line railway viaduct and, as you ascend, views to Bradford and Leeds beyond. White poles mark the route.

As the path levels off, cross a fairway, and continue ahead between two copses of trees. Emerge from the trees and cross a tarmac path to take a path ahead with a large barn on your right and continue past Lunds Farm on your right. At a path junction, where the main track swings to the left, go straight ahead along a grassy path. Keep ahead on a grassy woodland path with a wall on your right. As you emerge from the woodland with a golf tee on your left, turn right off the path through a gap in the wall, on a signposted path (white marker post). Follow this path downhill with a wall on your right and after 75 yards (SE 171408) turn sharp left to cross diagonally to a gap in the wall. Go through the gap and continue downhill following the white marker posts, keeping the boundary hedge on the left, to the walls of Hollins Hall Hotel.

(Refreshment may be obtained at the far end of the hotel in the Country Club).

Continue ahead past the hotel, downhill, with a stone wall on your left and a small coppice on your right, to a road. Follow the yellow Public Footpath roundel arrows and turn left through a galvanised iron gate towards a house and immediately right down a drive with a garage on your right again following the Public Footpath yellow arrows. Continue downhill over the railway bridge to Hollins Hill.

30. Cross the very busy Hollins Hill with great care to continue down a bridleway, signposted Cunliffe Lane. The bridleway becomes a paved road as it brings you into Esholt. After passing through the attractive open area of Bunker's Hill at the end of Cunliffe Lane, turn left on the pavement alongside a road to reach Esholt village.

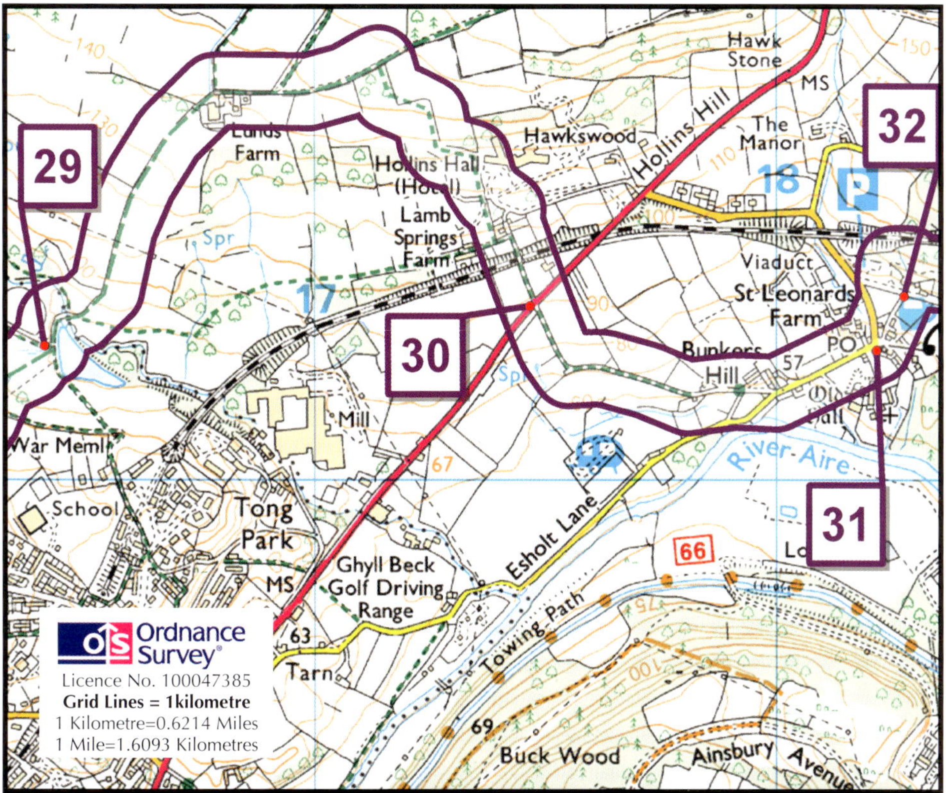

Near Lund's Farm

12. Esholt to Guiseley 1.6 miles

31. Just after the junction of Chapel Lane, Church Lane, Station Road, and Main Street (playground down to the right) cross the road towards the Woolpack and bear left to ascend a public footpath signposted Pullen Lane with allotments to your right.

32. At the path T-junction, turn left on the road and very soon turn right to ascend into woodland. Go up to and through a kissing gate and turn right to cross two wooden footbridges and take the main track, contouring and rising gently, with houses below to your right, towards Esholt sewage works, and then to a new plantation of young trees. Continue ahead through a gateway in a crenellated wall. After 100 yards enter a conifer plantation, and, at a path junction, take the left fork which rises with increasing steepness uphill. Keep to the main track as it bears left to reach the hill crest, cross a track and continue in the same direction (NE). Descend to cross a small stream and rise up the other side, following the main track as it veers left. The track then turns right downhill with a deep railway cutting on the left to reach a footbridge over Guiseley Beck at the bottom.

33. Cross the footbridge and follow the stream left. At a muddy cross track, turn left across a stone bridge and immediately pass under a railway bridge. Continue uphill initially on a broad track between stone walls but soon turn right off this track, through a steel gate, across an open field beneath power-lines. Continue on the path ahead (railway line now to your right). Cross a tarmac road and continue ahead along a ginnel between wooden panel fencing. At the end of the ginnel turn right on pavements through a housing estate road towards Guiseley. Where the road swings left and uphill, turn right into a small cul-de-sac to join a Public Footpath sign sporting a Yorkshire Rose. At the end of this footpath enter a busy main road junction. Use the light controlled pedestrian crossing to reach Aireborough Leisure Centre.

Spring Wood, near Esholt

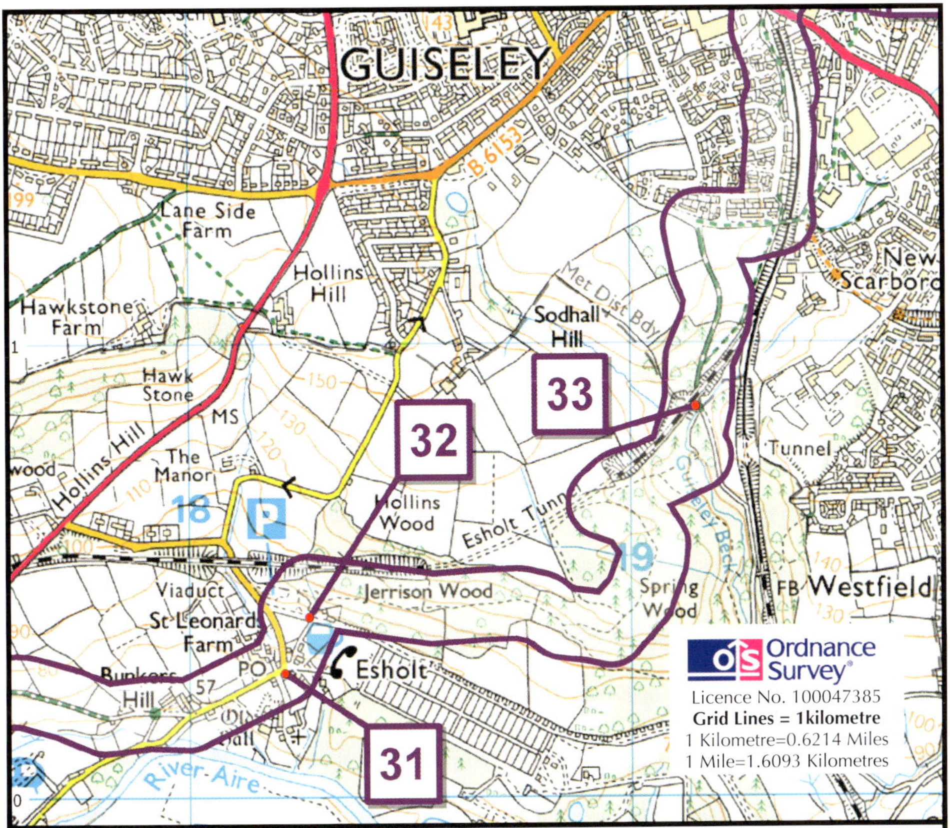

Woolpack at Esholt

13. Guiseley to Royalty Public House 2.0 miles

34. From Aireborough Leisure Centre continue northwards up The Green as far as St Oswald's Church on the right. Turn right on Church Street for 200 yards to reach a ginnel on the left. Turn left and through the ginnel to reach Queensway.

35. Cross Queensway to the ladder stile opposite. Go over the ladder stile and continue forward to reach a track, turn left for 50 yards to a stile on the right. Go over the stile into a field and follow the stream on the right over several stiles and around a number of corners to a track junction at SE 203428 reached after a slight decline from some large trees . Turn left here into an enclosed path. Follow this path for 200 yards to a farm access track. Turn left here and follow the track to the road.

36. Turn right on the road (Carlton Lane) for 250 yards to an access bridleway on the left. Turn left here and follow this bridleway northwards to a sharp left turn. Turn right here through a gate and into a field. Turn left after fifty yards and go up the field to a stile in the wall. Go over the stile and turn left to another stile at the north side of the field. Cross and follow this footpath until you reach the Royalty Public House on Otley Chevin.

Royalty Public House on Otley Chevin

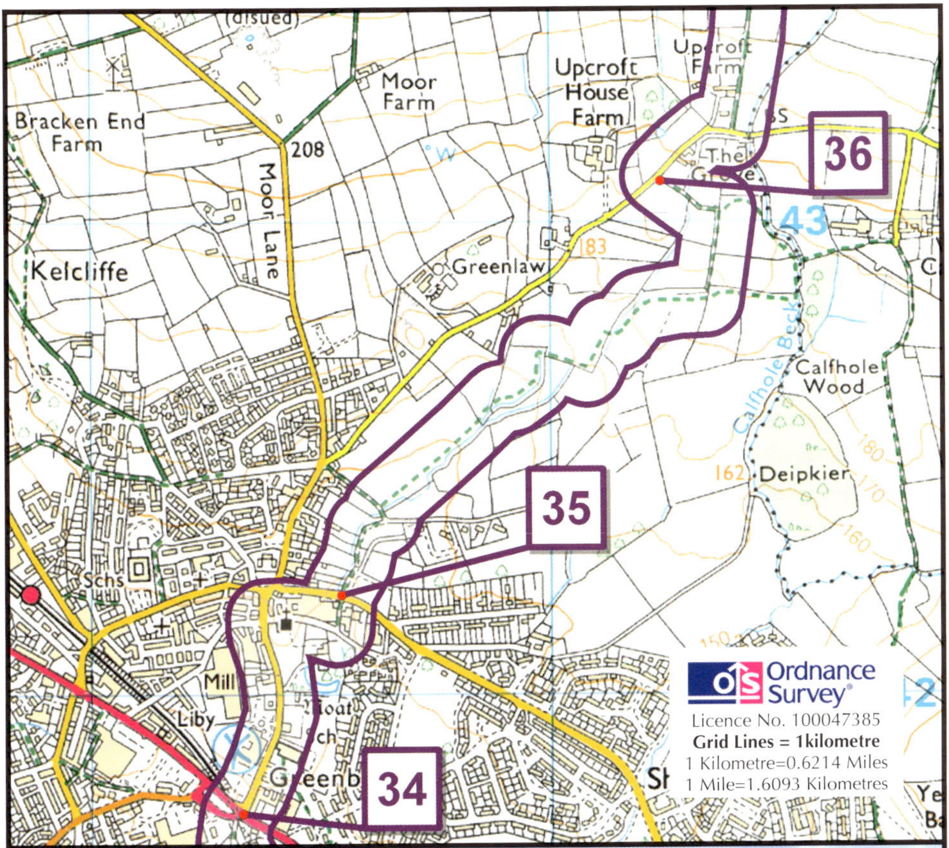

Footpath near Guiseley

WELCOME TO OTLEY

Welcome to the historic market town of Otley in West Yorkshire, one of the three "Walkers are Welcome" towns where you may start or finish the WELCOME WAY walk.

Otley is a thriving town with a population of fourteen thousand plus. It has a beautiful setting beside the River Wharfe, below the wooded escarpment known as the Chevin. It has grown up at an important bridging point on the river.

At its heart are the cobbled market square, the "Buttercross" and the historic town clock. It lies at the centre of an important agricultural area.

Otley from the Chevin

The town has been a location for the film and TV industry for many years. As you wander the streets don't be surprised if you recognise scenes from Emmerdale, Heartbeat, the Chase and other programmes.

Otley is surrounded by spectacular countryside. In the valley an attractive riverside park leads on to paths and meadows. Above, the wooded slopes of the Chevin form a Country Park, which was donated to the people of Otley by the Fawkes family of nearby Farnley Hall. It is popular with walkers, strollers and climbers. There are many paths and rights of way leading out of Otley. It links to several long distance walks, being the starting point for the 38-mile Six Dales Trail from Otley to Middleham, and a stage on the new North East Leeds and Country Parks Greenways Trail. The Ebor Way and a Dales Way Link cross the Chevin.
At the end of June each year there is a highly popular nine-day Walking Festival with a wide choice of guided walks, [www.otleywalkingfestival.co.uk].

Jubilee Tower in Otley

Otley is a flourishing shopping location. The traditional street market takes place in the square and along Kirkgate on Tuesdays, Fridays and Saturdays, with fruit and vegetables, plants and clothes stalls amongst others. In addition there is a farmers market on the last Sunday of each month selling locally sourced produce, including plants, preserves, meats and baked goods.

Otley has a good range of shops, pubs and cafes. There are many local independent businesses as well as some national and regional chains. There are three supermarkets. Of significance to walkers is a shop selling an excellent range of outdoor clothing and equipment [www.chevintrek.co.uk].

Otley is noted for its number of traditional pubs serving both food and drink, including an excellent range of real ales [www.otleypubclub.co.uk]. There is also an excellent selection of daytime cafes, evening restaurants and takeaways. Breakfast, lunch, dinner, teas and coffees are all catered for. There is high quality accommodation in pubs and B&Bs in the town centre, with further accommodation a short drive or bus ride away. There is a local hospital north of the river with a minor injuries clinic.

Historical highlights

Otley grew up as a river crossing point, probably in Saxon times, although there are earlier (Bronze Age) traces of settlement in the area. The Archbishops of York were medieval Lords of the Manor and had a palace in Otley, the remains of which have been found near the site of the present "manor house" overlooking the river.

One of the most noteworthy historic buildings in the town is the seven span stone bridge across the river Wharfe, which has its origins at least as far back as the 13th century.

The Parish Church stands on high ground above Kirkgate. There are Anglo Saxon foundations on the site, and the remains of two ancient crosses. An 11th century Norman church forms the present chancel. A wide nave, transepts and simple tower were added in the 13th century and further additions and alterations over the centuries have resulted in the present, attractive stone building.

The market began with a charter granted by Henry III in 1222 and Otley was a significant medieval town as demonstrated by the way routes radiate from it. Otley went on to expand during the 19th century industrial revolution when initially the river and later coal and steam were used to power mills. Only a few of these are still standing, mainly to the west of the town. The waters of the river still flow over the weirs used to pond back and divert the water for the mills and a tannery. Paper making and printing machinery manufacture were important alongside the usual Yorkshire woollen and worsted mills. The Wharfedale printing machine was developed and made in Otley. It revolutionised printing.

Thomas Chippendale Statue in Otley

Otley's street pattern, centred on the market square, has hints of its medieval origin with some visible burgage plots, closes and crofts. Further out are the terraced cottages of the industrial workers. Today the town has many newer housing estates with expansion north of the river. Many people now work in Leeds. The modern day shops are built onto much older buildings some of which are better seen by exploring the narrow cobbled streets and alleys that lead off the main thoroughfares.

Thomas Chippendale the famous furniture maker was born in the town in 1718 and his statue stands outside the attractive building that was the original Grammar School. Examples of his work can be found in nearby country houses.

The artist JMW Turner was a frequent visitor to nearby Farnley Hall and Otley's countryside is believed to have inspired several of his paintings including "Hannibal crossing the Alps!"

In the cobbled alley next to the church there is a memorial to twenty three "navvies" who died in the building of the nearby Bramhope railway tunnel in the 1840s

Find out more about Otley

Otley public library and tourist information centre:
www.otleytowncouncil.gov.uk/otley/tourist-information/
Visit Otley: www.visitotley.co.uk
Walkers are Welcome, Otley have produced leaflets of self-guided local walks, available in local shops. [www.waw-otley.org]

Public Transport

Otley has regular bus services to Leeds (X84), Harrogate (X52 and 762), Keighley (762), Ilkley (X84, X52 and 762) and Skipton (X84) and the shuttle bus 967 runs to Leeds Bradford Airport and to Menston railway station, which links to the national rail network in Leeds.
www.wymetro.com

Approaching the White House, Otley Chevin

14. Royalty Public House to Otley 1.4 miles

37. Leave the Royalty car park and turn left to the Surprise View car park on the right. Go through the car park and exit through a wall onto the Chevin. Turn right here on a stone-flagged path which goes diagonally, sloping off to the left. Follow this downhill to reach a wide track.

38. Turn left and follow the wide track steeply downhill to reach the White House. Continue around the White House turning right on a wide vehicle track to exit onto a metalled road. Cross the road into an enclosed path and follow this downhill to reach another road.

39. Cross this road with care into another enclosed path which quickly reaches a footbridge over the Otley bypass. Go over the footbridge and into Station Road which leads into Otley. At the Parish Church continue ahead on Kirkgate to reach the finish at the Market Place in Otley.

Otley Parish Church

River Wharfe Bridge

Welcome Way - Bingley Loop

An outline map of the Welcome Way - Bingley Loop is detailed on the facing page.

The Loop may be started at any place on the route or linked into the Welcome Way detailed in this publication.

Starting from the centre of Bingley, the route leaves through Myrtle Park to cross the River Aire which it then follows via a road and riverside path downstream to Hirst Wood, which is just beyond the Shipley to Keighley rail line. The route then goes through the pleasant Hirst Wood to a car park on the outskirts of Saltaire. It then crosses the Leeds Liverpool Canal and re-crosses the River Aire before ascending up through the woods on Shipley Glen.

Bingley, Five Rise Locks
© Copyright Martin Clark

Here the route joins the main Welcome Way which it follows for just over a half mile until it then crosses Loadpit Beck to join Saltaire Road and exits onto Otley Road in Eldwick. From Eldwick the route uses tracks and paths to cross westwards to the outskirts of Bingley.
The route then follows an enclosed footpath to Micklethwaite Green before dropping down to cross and join the Leeds Liverpool Canal.
The canal towpath is then followed to pass the Five Rise Locks and reach the footbridge which crosses the Aire Valley Trunk Road and the rail line in Bingley to reach Bingley High Street and the finish.

Map reading skills may be used to follow the map on the facing page or futher details of this route in leaflet form may be obtained from WAW in Bingley or the Visitor Centre on Shipley Glen.

Buses and train links are available in Bingley and Bracken Hall Visitor Centre is serviced by a bus link from Baildon and Shipley.

Green End
Belle Vue
Carr House Farm
Hebble Bridge
Prospect House
Drake Hill
The Riggs
Graincliffe Reservoir
Intake Wood
Eldwick Crag Farm
Mount Hill
Crag
Toils Farm
Peas Acre
High Fold
Micklethwaite
Morton Bridge (Swing)
Deer Park
Hill Top
Walsh Lane
Heights Lane
Low House
Compensation Reservoir
Eldwick Hall
Lane Head
Dales Way Link
Eldwick Beck
Laythorp Farm
Greenhill Farm
The Greenwood
Tewitt House
The Heights
Quarries (disused)
Cragg Wood Farm
Golcar Farm
The Springs
Low Fold Farm
Glovershaw Farm
Gloversha Beck
Nursing Home
Crossflatts
Eldwick
Prince of Wales Park
Waterfall
Swing Bridge
Five Rise Locks
Cemy
Bailey Hills
Priestthorpe
Crow Nest
Hospital
Sheriff Farm
Sheriff Lane
Glen Road
Mitton Spring
BINGLEY
Ferncliffe
Gilstead
Shipley Glen
Soldiers Trench
Myrtle
Resr
Airedale
Milnerfield Farm
Dowley Gap
Mills
Locks
Aqueduct
Hirst Wood
Weir
Beck Foot
Shipley Golf Club
Club House
Millennium Way
School
Rye Loaf Hill
Cemetery
Crem
Park Road
Round Hill
Cottingley Viaduct
Bankfield Hotel
Hospl
Nab Wood
A 650
B 6265
B 6146
Ordnance Survey
Licence No. 100047385
Grid Lines = 1kilometre
1 Kilometre=0.6214 Miles
1 Mile=1.6093 Kilometres

Acknowledgements

The Steering Group for this project is very grateful for the extensive support and encouragement that has been received from our local authorities, financial backers, graphic designers, printer, proof readers and photographers, all of whom have contributed to making the 'Welcome Way' a reality.

Kate Ashbrook, Patron
www.campaignerkate.wordpress.com

Walkers are Welcome

Baildon www.baildonwalkersarewelcome.org
Bingley www.bingleywalkersarewelcome.org.uk
Burley in Wharfedale www.waw-burleyinwharfedale.org
Otley www.waw-otley.org.uk

Otley Walkers
www.otleywalkers.webs.com

Ramblers Holiday Charitable Trust
http://opencharities.org/charities/1069835

Long Distance Walking Association
www.ldwa.org.uk

Bradford Tourism,
www.visitbradford.com

Nicky Bunting,
Public Rights of Way Officer,
www.northyorks.gov.uk

Ward Councillors
for Otley, Yeadon, Guiseley
and Rawdon
Roger Brooks, Parks and Countryside

Danny Jackson,
Countryside and Rights of Way,
City of Bradford Metropolitan
District Council
www.bradford.gov.uk